VOLUME 1

MW00598128

Solos for Young Violinists

Compiled and Edited by Violinist **Barbara Barber**

Contents

Violin by Joannes Franciscus Pressenda, Turin, 1846
from the collection of Robertson & Sons Violin Shop Incorporated, Albuquerque, NM

© 1997 Summy-Birchard Music
division of Summy-Birchard Inc.
Exclusive print rights administered by
Alfred Publishing Co., Inc.
All Rights Reserved   Printed in USA

ISBN 0-87487-988-4

INTRODUCTION

Solos for Young Violinists is a six volume series of music books with companion CDs featuring more than 50 pieces for violin and piano. Many of the works in this collection have long been recognized as stepping stones to the major violin repertoire, while others are newly published pieces which offer further choices for study; most are recorded in this series for the very first time. Compiled, edited and recorded by violinist Barbara Barber, *Solos for Young Violinists* is a graded series of works ranging from elementary to advanced levels and represents an exciting variety of styles and techniques for violinists. The collection has become a valuable resource for teachers and students of all ages. The piano track recorded on the second half of each CD gives the violinist the opportunity to practice with accompaniments.

Simple Folk Songs
for violin and piano
arranged by Barbara Barber

1. French Folk Song
Playing Ball on the Stairs

6

2. English Folk Song
The Old Woman and the Peddler

Allegretto ♩ = 64

Optional introduction

3. Bohemian Folk Song
November

Andante ♩ = 48

Optional introduction

rit.

rit.

4. Welsh Air

All Through the Night

5. French Folk Song

Good Pierrot

6. Bohemian Folk Song
Winter

7. Russian Folk Song

Caterpillar! Caterpillar!

8. Scotch Folk Song

Lullaby

Marche

J. S. Bach
Arranged by Constance Seely-Brown

Musette

J.S. Bach
Arranged by Constance Seely-Brown

Allegretto ♩ = 98

Giguetta

J.S. Bach
Arranged by Constance Seely-Brown

Theme and Variations

Guido Papini
Transcribed by Samuel Applebaum

18

Concertino in G Major
Op. 8, No. 4

Adolf Huber

Tempo I

Donkey Doodle

William Kroll

28

Elves Dance

E. Jenkinson

La Cinquantaine

Gabriel - Marie

The Puppet Show
Op. 5, No. 1

Josephine Trott

Mosquito Dance
Op. 62, No. 5

Ludwig Mendelssohn

Concertino in D Major
Op. 15
In the style of Antonio Vivaldi

Ferdinand Küchler

46